I Is a Long Memoried Woman

Grace Nichols

i is a long memoried woman
poetry
by Grace Nichols

2330836

© Grace Nichols 1983; reprinted 1984, 1986, 1990
All Rights Reserved

First published in Britain 1983
by Karnak House
300 Westbourne Park Road
London W11 1EH
UK

tel. 071.221.6490

Distributed in the USA
by The Red Sea Press
11-D Princess Road
Lawrenceville, N.J. 08648
U.S.A.
Tel: 609 844 9583
Fax: 609 844 0198

RSP

Photosetting by Emset, London NW10

British Library Cataloguing in Publication Data
Nichols, Grace 1950-
    i is a memoried woman
    I. Title
    811

ISBN 0-907015-67-0

Contents

(Part One) The Beginning   4
One Continent/To Another   5
Web of Kin   8
Days That Fell   10
We The Women   12
Waterpot   13
Each Time They Came   15
Eulogy   16
Taint   18
Sacred Flame   19
Sunshine   21

(Part Two) The Vicissitudes   22
Ala   23
Without Song   25
Among the Canes   27
Drum Spell   28
These Islands   31
Sugar Cane   32
I Go To Meet Him   36
One Dream   38

(Part Three) The Sorcery   39
. . . Like Clamouring Ghosts   40
I Coming Back   42
Hi De Buckras Hi!   43
Nimbus   45
Night Is Her Robe   46

Old Magic   47
Love Act   48
Skin Teeth   50

(Part Four) The Bloodling   51
Your Blessing   52
In My Name   56
The Wandering   58
Of Golden Gods   59
I Will Enter   61
Kanaima Jungle   63
Yemanji   64
The Return   65
Like Anansi   66
Dark Signs   68
New Birth   70

(Part Five) The Return   71
Nanny   72
Blow Winds Blow   74
This Kingdom   75
Wind A Change   78
Time Of Ogun/Mambu   80
Omen   81
. . .And Tossaint   83
I Cross Myself   85
Holding My Beads   86
Epilogue   87

From dih pout
of mih mouth
from dih
treacherous
calm of mih
smile
you can tell
i is a long memoried woman

THE BEGINNING

ONE CONTINENT/TO ANOTHER

Child of the middle passage womb
push
daughter of a vengeful Chi
she came
    into the new world
birth aching her pain
from one continent/to another

moaning

her belly cry sounding the wind

after fifty years
she hasn't forgotten
hasn't forgotten
how she had lain there
in her own blood
lain there in her own shit

bleeding memories in the darkness

how she stumbled onto the shore
how the metals dragged her down
how she thirsted . . . . .

But being born a woman
she moved again
knew it was the Black Beginning
though everything said it was
the end

And she went forth with others of her kind
to scythe the earth knowning that bondage
would not fall like poultice from the
children's forehead

But O she grieved for them
walking beadless
in another land

From the darkness within her
from the dimness of previous incarnations
    the Congo surfaced
so did Sierra Leone and the
Gold Coast which she used to tread
searching the horizons for lost
moons
her jigida guarding the crevice
the soft wet forest
    between her thighs

Like the yesterday of creation morning
she had imagined this new world to be —
bereft of fecundity

No she wasn't prepared
for the sea that lashed
fire that seared
solid earth that delivered
her up
birds that flew
not wanting to see the utter
rawness of life everywhere

and the men who seed the children
she wasn't prepared for that look
in their eye

that loss of deep man pride

Now she stoops
in green canefields
piecing the life she would lead

WEB OF KIN

I come from the Season-of-Locusts
from scorch of sun
and days of endless raining

from the sea that washes the Ivory Coast
I come from coral reefs
from distant tum-tum pounding

from muddy rivers
from long and twisting niger-rivers
I come from web of kin
from sacred new yam reapings

I come from a country of strong women
Black Oak women who bleed slowly at
the altars of their children
because mother is supreme
  burden

Still, at nights the women come
bearing gourds of sacrificial blood —
the offering of their silent woman
suffering

I will have nothing to do with it
will pour it in the dust will set
us free
the whip will have no fire the sun
no flame
and my eyes everywhere reflecting

even in dreams I will submerge myself
swimming like one possessed
back and forth across that course
strewing it with sweet smelling
flowers
one for everyone who made the journey

and at evenings I will recline
hair full of sun
    hands full of earth
I will recline on my bed of leaves
bid the young ones enter sit them
all around me

feed them sweet tales of Dahomey

DAYS THAT FELL

And yet . . . . .
And yet . . . . .

the cutlass in her hand
could not cut through
the days that fell
like bramble

and the destruction that
threatened to choke
within

as she leaned closer to
the earth
seeking some truth
unarmed against the noon

We must hold fast to dreams
We must be patient
from the crouching of those huts
from the sprouting of these fields
We can emerge

all revolutions are rooted in dreams

And yet . . . . .
And yet . . . . .

the cutlass in her hand
could not cut through
the days that fell
like bramble

and the destruction that
threatened to choke within

as she leaned close to
the earth
seeking some truth
unarmed against the noon

WE THE WOMEN

We the women who toil
unadorn
heads tie with cheap
cotton

We the women who cut
clear fetch dig sing

We the women making
something from this
ache-and-pain-a-me
back-o-hardness

Yet we the women
whose praises go unsung
whose voices go unheard
whose deaths they sweep
aside
as easy as dead leaves

WATERPOT

The daily going out
and coming in
always being hurried
along
like like...cattle

In the evenings
returning from the fields
she tried hard to walk
like a woman

she tried very hard
pulling herself erect
with every three or four
steps
pulling herself together
holding herself like royal cane

And the overseer
hurrying them along
in the quickening darkness

And the overseer sneering
them along in the quickening
darkness

sneered at the pathetic —
the pathetic display
of dignity

O but look
there's a waterpot growing
from her head

EACH TIME THEY CAME

Igbo/Yoruba
Ashanti/Fanti
Mane

each time they came
she went out to see
them
the new arrivals
faces full of old
incisions
calves grooved from
shackles
ankles swollen
from the pain

Each time they came
she made
as if to touch them
the new arrivals
her own lips
moving in a dreaming
kind of prayer

EULOGY

Everywhere I hear them whispering
in ruptured tones of nostalgia
voices pushed in by the sea breeze
darting like pains in my head

cadances like the living
  parables of the dead

Yes the souls
Yes the souls
Yes the souls
caught in the Middle Passage
limbo

the dead ones
who are not dead
the sleeping ones
who are not sleeping

the restless ones

the leaping suicide
ones . . . . . the saddest
ones of all who toss and
moan
with each lash of the ocean
foam

Everywhere I hear them whispering
in ruptured tones of nostalgia
voices pushed in by the sea breeze
darting like pains in my head

cadances like the living
parables of the dead

Yes the souls
Yes the souls
Yes the souls
caught in the Middle Passage
limbo

How can I eulogise
their names?
What dance of mourning
can I make?

How can I eulogise
their names?
What dance of mourning
can I make?

Dayadu, Ishiodu, Anamadi
plunging wildly to the waters
of your fate
Kobidja, Nwasobi, Okolie
swallowing your tongues
cold and still on your chains

How can I eulogise your names
What dance of mourning can I make?

17

TAINT

But I was stolen by men
the colour of my own skin
borne away by men whose heels
had become hoofs
whose hands had turned talons
bearing me down
    to the trail
of darkness

But I was traded by men
the colour of my own skin
traded like a fowl   like a goat
like a sack of kernels I was
traded
    for beads   for pans
for trinkets?

No it isn't easy to forget
what we refuse to remember

Daily I rinse the taint
of treachery from my mouth

SACRED FLAME

Our women
the ones I left behind
always know the taste
of their own strength —
bitter at times it might
be

But I
armed only with
my mother's smile
must be forever gathering
my life together like scattered beads

What was your secret mother —
the one that made you a woman
and not just Akosu's wife

With your thighs you gave
a generation of beautiful children

With your mind you willed the crops
commanding a good harvest

With your hands and heart
plantain soup and love

19

But the sacred flame of your woman's
kra you gave to no man, mother

Perhaps that was the secret then —
the one that made you a woman
and not just Akosu's wife

SUNSHINE

Sun shine
with as bright a flame
here
there is red and gold
profusions
   in the green
of foliage

there is bird song

but where're our shrines?
      where're our stools?
         How shall I worship
            How shall I walk
               from now on?

the truth is
   my life has slipped out
      of my possession

THE VICISSITUDES

ALA

Face up
they hold her naked body
to the ground
arms and legs spread-eagle
each tie with rope to stake

then they coat her in sweet
molasses and call us out
to see . . . . . the rebel woman

who with a pin
stick the soft mould
of her own child's head

sending the little-new-born
soul winging its way back
to Africa — free

they call us out to see
the fate for all us rebel
women

the slow and painful
picking away of the flesh
by red and pitiless ants

but while the ants feed
and the sun blind her with
his fury
we the women sing and weep
as we work

O Ala
Uzo is due to join you
to return to the pocket
of your womb

Permit her remains to be
laid to rest — for she has
died a painful death

O Ala
Mother who gives and receives
again in death
Gracious one
have sympathy
let her enter
let her rest

WITHOUT SONG

The faces of the children
    are small and stricken and black
They have fallen
into exile
moving without song
or prayer

They have fallen
into mourning
moving to the shrouds
of tares

The faces of the children
    are small and stricken and black

They have fallen
into silence
uttering no cry
laying no blame

And the sun burns to copper
yet the rains, the rains gather
like diamonds
in the fleece of their hair

Maybe the thing is to forget
to forget and be blind
on this little sugar island

to forget the Kingdom of Ancestors
the washing of throats with palm wine

to not see that woman, female flesh
feast coated in molasses

Maybe the thing is to forget
to forget and be blind
on this little sugar island

AMONG THE CANES

Like the cyclic blood
that snaps within her
so too her faith
flowing
  in darkness   across the fields
now she's over-run
by the mice of despair

O who will remember me?
Who will remember me? she wails
holding her belly
stumbling blindly
among the canes

O like my Earth Mother
Asaase Yaa
I demand a day of rest

DRUM-SPELL

Suddenly, for no reason
though there is reason
plenty
I feel the dizzying
        mid-day
        drum-spell
        come over me

        the melting
        hotness
        of my blood

        the cutlass
        slipping
        slowly

        the drum-beat
        rising
        faintly

Now I'm child
again walking small
and careful among the
mounds of my mother's yams
. . . . .the shoots of her hope-
fulness. . . . .the roots of
her despair

28

Now I see my father
nimble, catlike crouching
with his spear
    And I am between
    in the very heart
    of the days
    of blood and sacrificial
    slaughter

    the sunset offerings
    the feasts
    and gatherings
    the feeding of the
    hungry dead
    the ritual yam sprinkling

O once again
I am walking
roots
that are easy

Once again
I am talking
words
that come smoothly

Once again
I am in the eyes
of my sisters
they have not
forgotten my name

Osee yei yee yei
Osee yei yee yei

they cry from behind
their evening pots

rejoice!
rejoice!
rejoice!

she is back
she is back
she is back

Waye saa aye saa oo!
Waye saa aye saa oo!

She has done so
She has done so
She has done so

Mother behold
your wilful daughter

Yes the one who ventured
beyond our village is back

Osee yei yee yei
Osee yei yee yei

THESE ISLANDS

These islands green
   with green blades
these islands green
   with blue waves
these islands green
   with flame shades

these cane dancing
   palm waving wind
blowing islands
these sea growing
   mangroving
hurricane islands

these blue mountain islands
these fire flying islands
these Carib   bean
Arawak   an
islands
fertile
   with brutaility

SUGAR CANE

1
There is something
about sugarcane

He isn't what
he seem —

indifferent hard
and sheathed in blades

his waving arms
is a sign for help

his skin thick
only to protect
the juice inside
himself

2
His colour
is the aura
of jaundice
when he ripe
he shiver

like ague
when it rain

he suffer
from bellywork
burning fever
and delirium

just before
the hurricane
strike
smashing him to pieces

3
Growing up
is an art

he don't have
any control of

it is us
who groom and weed him

who stick him
in the earth
in the first place

and when he
growing tall

with the help
of the sun
and rain

we feel the
need to strangle
the life

out of him
But either way he can't survive

33

4
Slowly
pain-
fully
sugar
cane
pushes
his
knotted
joints
upwards
from
the
earth
slowly
pain-
fully
he
comes
to learn
the
truth
about
himself
the
crimes
committed
in
his
name

5

He cast his shadow
to the earth

the wind is
his only mistress

I hear them
moving
in rustling tones

she shakes
his hard reserve

smoothing
stroking
caressing
all his length
shamelessly

I crouch
below them
quietly

I GO TO MEET HIM

Mornings of dew
and promises

the sound
of brid singing

pink and red
hibiscus kissing

I must devote
sometime to the
joy of living

Raising up
from my weeding
of ripening cane

my eyes
make four
with this man

there ain't
no reason
to laugh

but
I laughing
in confusion

his hands
soft his words
quick his lips
curling as in
prayer

I nod

I like this man

Tonight
I go to meet him
like a flame

I see
the trembling star
of murder
in your palm
black man

bleeding
and raging
to death
inside yourself

broken and twisted
as a wheel
watching your blood
run
    thin and saltless
to the earth
as you grip the throat of cane

kin of my skin you are

ONE DREAM

I must construct myself a dreaam
one dream is all I need to keep
me from the borders of this darkness

I must construct myself a dream
one dream is all I need to keep
me from these blades of hardness

from this plague of sadness

This Dream Must Not Be Tarnished

THE SORCERY

...LIKE CLAMOURING GHOSTS

Last Night I dream a terrible
dream
I dream about the gods forcing
me to drink blood from my father
skull
forcing me to eat dirt

And when I try to run the chiefs
and elders of the tribe come after
me like clamouring ghosts

In this dream I see my own face
wild and greyish with terror

What hope have I if the old ones
turn against me in my dreams

I see the old dry-head woman
leaning on her hoe
twist-up and shaky like a cripple
insect

I see her ravaged skin, the stripes
of mold where the whip fall
hard

I see her missing toe, her jut-out
hipbone from way back time when
she had a fall

I see the old dry-head woman
leaning on her hoe
twist-up and shaky like a cripple
insect

I see the pit of her eye

I hear her rattle bone laugh
putting a chill up my spine

Once she too was woman
clad
in her loveliest woman
skin gleaming faintly
with oils breasts nippling
the wind

I COMING BACK

I coming back "Massa"
I coming back

mistress of the underworld
I coming back

colour and shape
of all that is evil
I coming back

dog howling outside
yuh window
I coming back

ball-a-fire
and skinless higue
I coming back

hiss in yuh ear
and prick in yuh skin
I coming back

bone in yuh throat
and laugh in yuh skull
I coming back

I coming back "Massa"
I coming back

HI DE BUCKRAS HI!

Vexation of mind
Vexation of eye
Vexation of spirit

Vexation of mind
Vexation of eye
Vexation of spirit

Look at the buckra woman
head in parasol floating
by white and pale
being helped from carriages
being lifted over ditches
floating by white and pale
not even looking
not even seeing
the pain and rage and black
despair

Vexation on mind
Vexation of eye
Vexation of spirit

Vexation of mind
Vexation of eye
Vexation of spirit

(Bursts into song)

O buckra woman she come over de sea
with she round blue eyes from she
cold countree

She walk straight, she head high
she too fenky
she better take care she don't turn
zombie

O buckra man him come over de sea
with him pluck-chicken skin
from him cold countree

Him palaver him a pray him a dress
fancee but suddenly so him turning
weak and dizzy

O buckra woman she come over de sea
with she round blue eyes from she cold
countree

She walk straight she head high
she too fenky
she better take care she don't
turn zombie

She better take care she don't
turn zombie

Hi de buckras hi
Hi de buckras hi
Hi de buckras hi
O Hi de buckras hi!

NIMBUS

Sitting in the shadows
countering darkness/
with darkness
fingers caught
in the rhythmic
braiding of her
hair

room infused with
lavender
and the nimbus
growing from herself

Listen
hear her laughter
soft and harsh
in the darkness

NIGHT IS HER ROBE

Night is her robe
Moon is her element

Quivering and alert
she's stepping out behind
the fields of sugarcane

She's stepping out softly
she's stepping out carefully
she's bending/she's stalking
she's fitting/she's crawling

Quivering and alert
she's coming to the edge
of her island forest

Now with all the care
of a herbalist
she's gathering strange weeds
wild root
leaves with the property
both to harm and to heal

Quivering and alert
Quivering and alert
she's leaving the edge
of her island forest

OLD MAGIC

She, the mirror
you break in seven pieces

the curse you think
you leave behind

the woman make young
with old magic

the one you going
sleep with

the one you going
think is kind

LOVE ACT

She enter into his Great House
her see-far looking eyes
unassuming

He fix her with his glassy stare
and feel the thin fire in his blood
awakening

Soon she is the fuel
that keep them all going

He/his mistresswife/and his
children who take to her breasts
like leeches

he want to tower above her
want her to raise her ebony
haunches and when she does
he thinks she can be trusted
and drinks her in

And his mistresswife
spending her days in rings
of vacant smiling
is glad to be rid of the
loveact

But time pass/es

Her sorcery cut them
like a whip

She hide her triumph
and slowly stir the hate
of poison in

SKIN TEETH

Not every skin-teeth
is a smile "Massa"

if you see me smiling
when you pass

if you see me bending
when you ask

Know that I smile
know that I bend
only the better
to rise and strike
again

THE BLOODLING

. . . . . .YOUR BLESSING

Aie
the very first
time she knew
she was carrying
she wanted to
cry out

her throat
was a fist
of fear

she wanted
to crush
the weaving
blood mystery

to retch
herself
empty

days passed
she resigned
herself to
silence

eye water
trickling
down
her
face

Cover me with the leaves of your
blackness Mother

shed tears

for I'm tainted with guilt and
exile

I'm burden with child and maim

Heal me with the power of your blackness
Mother

shed tears

for I'm severed by ocean and
longing

I'm mocked I'm torn I fear

Cover me
Heal me
Shield me

With the power of your blessings

Uplift me
Instruct me
Reclothe me

With the power of your blessings

Mother I need I crave your blessing
Mother I need I crave your blessing

Mother I hear your voice
I hear it far away
breaking the wildness of my
thoughts
calming me to childhood presence
once again

As we have known Victory
As we have known Death
As we have known —
neither to rely on happiness
nor sorrow for our existence

So rise you up my daughter

Mother I need I crave your blessing
Mother I need I crave your blessing

Like the bamboo cane that groans
and creeks in the wind. . . . .
but doesn't break

Like the drumskin that is beaten
on the outside. . . . . .
but keeps its bottom whole

So be you my daughter

Cast your guilt to the wind
Cast your trials to the lake
Clasp your child to your bosom
Give your exile to the snake

Mother I need I crave your blessing
Mother I need I crave your blessing

By the drumming of rain
and the running of stream
by the beating of sun
and the flash of steel
by the ripple of flesh
and despairing of dream

Heal, my daughter, heal

By the hot sun's eye
and the green cane stalk
by the root of blade
and the sweat of mind

Heal

cast your guilt to the wind
Cast your trials to the lake
Clasp your child to your bosom
Give your exile to the snake

Mother I need I have your blessing
Mother I need I have your blessing

IN MY NAME

Heavy with child

belly
an arc
of black moon

I squat over
dry plantain leaves

and command the earth
to receive you

im my name
in my blood

to receive you
my curled bean

my tainted
perfect child

                    my bastard fruit
                    my seedling
                    my sea grape
                    my strange mulatto
                    my little bloodling

Let the snake slipping in deep grass
be dumb before you

Let the centipede writhe and shrivel
in its tracks

Let the evil one strangle on his own tongue
even as he sets his eyes upon you

For with my blood
I've cleansed you
and with my tears
I've pooled the river Niger

now my sweet one it is for you to swim

THE WANDERING

Spirit of Sky
Spirit of Sea
Spirit of Stone
Spirit of Tree
Spirit that lurk in all things
is at one with me

OF GOLDEN GODS

Alone
skull as empty as a gobi
I watch my chameleon spirit
take its exit
shapely as a distant breeze
across the face of heaven

deepening
from azure
to indigo darkness
circling slowly the
archipelago
of burnished green

moving from land to sea
from swamp to Southern
vastness
where the rains have been
falling hardest
in the pit of the serpent jungle

up, past the Inca ruins
and back again
drifting onto Mexican plains

the crumbling of golden gods
the Aztec rites
speak for themselves
that, and before, the
genocides —
all a prelude to my time

And the darkness falls like rain
over Bolivian highlands

I WILL ENTER

Singed by a flight of scarlet ibises
blinded like a grasshopper by the rains

tattered and hungry
you took me in

gave me cassava bread
and casirri

a hammock to sleep in

a blanket woven by
your own hands
rich with embroidery

I will enter   into you
I will enter   into you
                  woman

through the Indian forest
of your hair
I will enter

through the passage of your
wary watchful eyes
I will enter

61

through the bitterness
of your cassava touch
I will enter

and when you are moonsick
I will bleed with you

But wait
like a broken flute
your tongue is silent
your eyes speak of an
ancient weariness
I too have known
memory is written
in each crumpled fold
you can still remember
how they pitted gun against
arrow
steel against stillness

Stunned by their demands
for gold

And so you'll talk no more
of *Amalivaca*
or the mystery of his strange
rock writings

No more of Kaie
brave old chief who took
to sacrifice on behalf
of his tribe
rushing the falls before
the great *Mokonima's* eye

KANAIMA JUNGLE

Everywhere I'm ensnared
by jungle

Rorimas of jungle
battalions of jungle
plateaux, valleys, dominions
of jungle

I can't cut through this jungle

maze of jungle
waterfall and climb
and haze of jungle

I can't cut through this jungle

prey of jungle
vampire and bird
and snake of jungle

I can't cut through this jungle

Gold-in-the river-bed of jungle
Diamonds-in-the-river-bed of jungle

I can't cut through this *kanaima* jungle

YEMANJI

It was here by the riverside
I came upon *Yemanji*
Mother of all beings sprawled
upon the rivershore, her long
breasts (insulted by her husband)
oozing milk that lapped and flowed

Yemanji
Mother of seas
Goddess of rivers
I will pay homage to you
you who bless your followers
with an abundance of children
you whose temple rests like a lotus
in Ibandan, you whose waters flow down
the River Ogun, past the cities of Abeokuta
and Oyo

Yemanji
Mother of Shango
Mother of the long breasts
of milk and sorrow

Sacred be your river stones

THE RETURN

Is that you Nanny
Is that you Black Priestess
Is that your Abeng voice
echoing its warcry through the valleys?

LIKE ANANSI

I was the Ashanti spider

woman-keeper
of dreams
tenacious
opalescent
dark eyes
unblinking

waiting
with a long
and naked fury

then you came
like Anansi
you came

calm and cunning
as a madman

not at all
what I was expecting

bells hung
from your little waist
an ornate flute

beads and feathers
stood in your cap
and I laughed at you

DARK SIGN

Yet even now
the Gods of my people
grow cold, turning
with anger

I have not forgotten
them
I have not forsaken
them

But I must be true
to the dark sign
of my woman's nature
to the wildness of my
solitude and exile

Circles round the moon
I can feel

hurricane months
fast coming

can see

tempestuous gathering
her rains and winds around
her like howling children

can see

palms rooting closer
to the earth

NEW BIRTH

Looking into the cascade
of foam
she saw that the hurricane
months had passed

that the air was quickened
with the taste of new birth
and the benediction of the sun

that the frogs were singing
from deep among the mangrove roots

The sun is singing
     the sky is singing
         I am singing into the day
             moving
beyond
     all   boundaries

THE RETURN

NANNY

Ashanti Priestess
and giver of charms
earth substance woman
of science
and black fire magic

Maroonic woman
of courage
and blue mountain rises

Standing over the valleys
dressed in purple robes
bracelets of the enemy's teeth
curled around your ankles
in rings of ivory bone

And your voice giving
sound to the Abeng
its death cry chilling
the mountainside
which you inhabit
like a strong pursuing eagle

As you watch the hissing
foaming cauldron
spelling strategies
for the red oppressors' blood
willing them to come
mouthing a new beginning song

Is that you Nanny — Is that you Nanny?

BLOW WINDS BLOW

Yes ancestral winds blow
O ancestral winds blow
stirring the dust of discontent

unrestful rumblings
shadowy meetings

drumprayers to Vaudoux
in darkforest clearing
                    Toussaint!
somebody
    tell me what happening

THIS KINGDOM

This Kingdom Will Not Reign
Forever

Cool winds blow
softly

in brilliant sunshine
fruits pulse
flowers flame

mountains shade to
purple

the great House
with its palm and orange
groves
sturdy

and the sea encircling
all
is a spectrum of blue
jewels
shimmering and skirting

But Beware

Soft winds can turn
volatile
can merge with rains
can turn hurricane

Mountains can erupt
sulphur springs
bubbling quick
and hot

like bile spilling
from a witch's cauldron

Swamps can send plagues
dysentry, fevers

plantations can perish

lands turn barren

And the white man
no longer at ease
with the faint drum/
beat

no longer indifferent
to the sweating sun/
heat

can leave exhausted
or
turn his thoughts
to death

And we
the rage growing
like the chiggers
in our feet

can wait
or
take our freedom

whatever happens

*This Kingdom Will Not Reign
Forever*

WIND A CHANGE

Wind a change
blow soft but
steadfast

ripple the spears
of sugar cane
stir slow the leaves
of indigo

Dance
waltz
soothe
this old mud-wattle
hut
bring if you can
the smell of Dahomey
again

Wind a change
cool mountain water
open river flower

But pass easy
up the big house
way
let them sleep
they happy white sleep

Yes, Wind a change
keep yuh coming fire
secret

TIME OF OGUN/MAMBU

It is almost upon us
the time of *Ogun*

the time of the
hard iron

of the cutlass
swiping its death scythe
across the earth

It is almost upon us —
the time of the *mambu*

dancing her earth shaking
dance
blood spilling
from the headless cockrel

OMEN

I require an omen, a signal
I kyan not work this craft
on my own strength
on my own strength

alligator teeth
and feathers
old root and powder

I kyan not work this craft
this magic black
on my own strength

Dahomey lurking in my shadows
Yoruba lurking in my shadows
Ashanti lurking in my shadows

I am confused
I lust for guidance
a signal, a small omen
perhaps a bird picking
at my roof

All is silent now
silent the fields
silent the canes
silent the drum
silent the blades
silent the sea
turning back to silence
a fatalistic rising silence

What's that sound/What's that flame?

.....AND TOUSSAINT

It has come
It has come

Fireritual
and bloodfeast
a banner of heads on spikes
the black surge

                and Toussaint in
                the Fort de Jour
                dying with cold

It has come
It has come

Firestorm
and bloodrage
a sky of flame
the black surge

                and Toussaint in
                the Fort de Jour
                dying with cold

It has come
It has come

Fireceremony
and bloodrush
an insane sunrise
the black surge

                              and Toussaint in
                              the Fort de Jour
                              dying with cold

It has come
It has come

Ashes to Ashes
Blood to Dust

Ashes to Ashes
Blood to Dust

                              and Toussaint in
                              the Fort de Jour
                              dying with hope

I CROSS MYSELF

Under the scarlet blossoms
of the poincianas
there are bodies.....
quite headless

I cross myself
I sprinkle the waters of purification
I close the eyes of the children with my lips
I lead them quickly away

HOLDING MY BEADS

Unforgiving as the course of justice
Inerasable as my scars and fate
I am here
a woman . . . . . with all my lives
strung out like beads
                              before me
It isn't privilege or pity
that I seek
It isn't reverence or safety
quick happiness or purity
                              but
the power to be what I am/a woman
charting my own futures/   a woman
holding my beads in my hand

EPILOGUE

I have crossed an ocean
I have lost my tongue
from the root of the old
one
a new one has sprung